POEMS

Faith, Giggles, & More

Copyright © by Patricia Malinchak

All rights reserved. No part of this book may be used or reproduced in any manner whatsoever without written permission, except in the case of brief quotations in critical articles and reviews. For more information, contact art.in.words.pm@gmail.com.

ISBN 979-8-218-75418-1   (print | paperback)

Published by Salt Water Media
29 Broad Street, Suite 104
Berlin, Maryland 21811
www.saltwatermedia.com

Cover Design, Layout, & Editorial Review by:
Pathway Writings, LLC
www.pathwaywritings.com

A variation of scripture quoted was taken from The Authorized (King James) Version. Rights in the Authorized Version in the United Kingdom are vested in the Crown. Reproduced by permission of the Crown's patentee, Cambridge University Press.

Interior images used with license by TextArt by book designer.

POEMS

Faith, Giggles, & More

Patricia Malinchak

Dedication

This book is dedicated to my lovely daughter,
who is a shining star in my life.

Contents

Introduction 11

Faith
    God's Gift 14
    A Christian in Faith 15
    To Jesus, With Love 16
    Forgiveness 17
    Faces 18
    Help Me 19
    Thoughts on the Lord's Prayer 20

Giggles
    The Fly in the Sky 24
    A Face in the Tree 25
    The Bright Light 26

& More
    Loneliness 28
    My Pond 29
    I Want to Be Free 30
    The Golden Years 31

Acknowledgements 33

Introduction

I have always been a frustrated artist. I tried singing and taking piano lessons, creating art with charcoal and oils, and decorating cakes. I finally discovered my true talent and niche when I began writing children's stories for my grandson.

The poem, "The Bright Light," originated when my forehead turned bright red after I had applied topical chemo on it.

Faith

God's Gift

Cloudy—then sunny and warm.
The trees dancing in the wind
To the melody of the pond's waterfall.
Snow-white clouds in the clear blue sky.
Green grass, colorful flowers.
Oh, what a gift for our souls.
Thank you, God.

A CHRISTIAN IN FAITH

WITH GOD'S INTERVENTION
I'M UNDER HIS PROTECTION.
THANKFUL FOR ALL THINGS
HE'S GIVEN TO ME.

MY LIFE GOES IN CYCLES
OF TEN YEARS OR MORE.
SOME HAVE BEEN RICH
AND SOME HAVE BEEN POOR.

THE GOOD TIMES ARE GREAT,
THE BAD TIMES, MY FATE.
GOD IS ALWAYS NEAR
WALKING WITH OR CARRYING ME.

EXPERIENCE HAS TAUGHT ME,
TO HAVE GREAT STRENGTH
PHYSICALLY AND MENTALLY,
AS A CHRISTIAN IN FAITH.

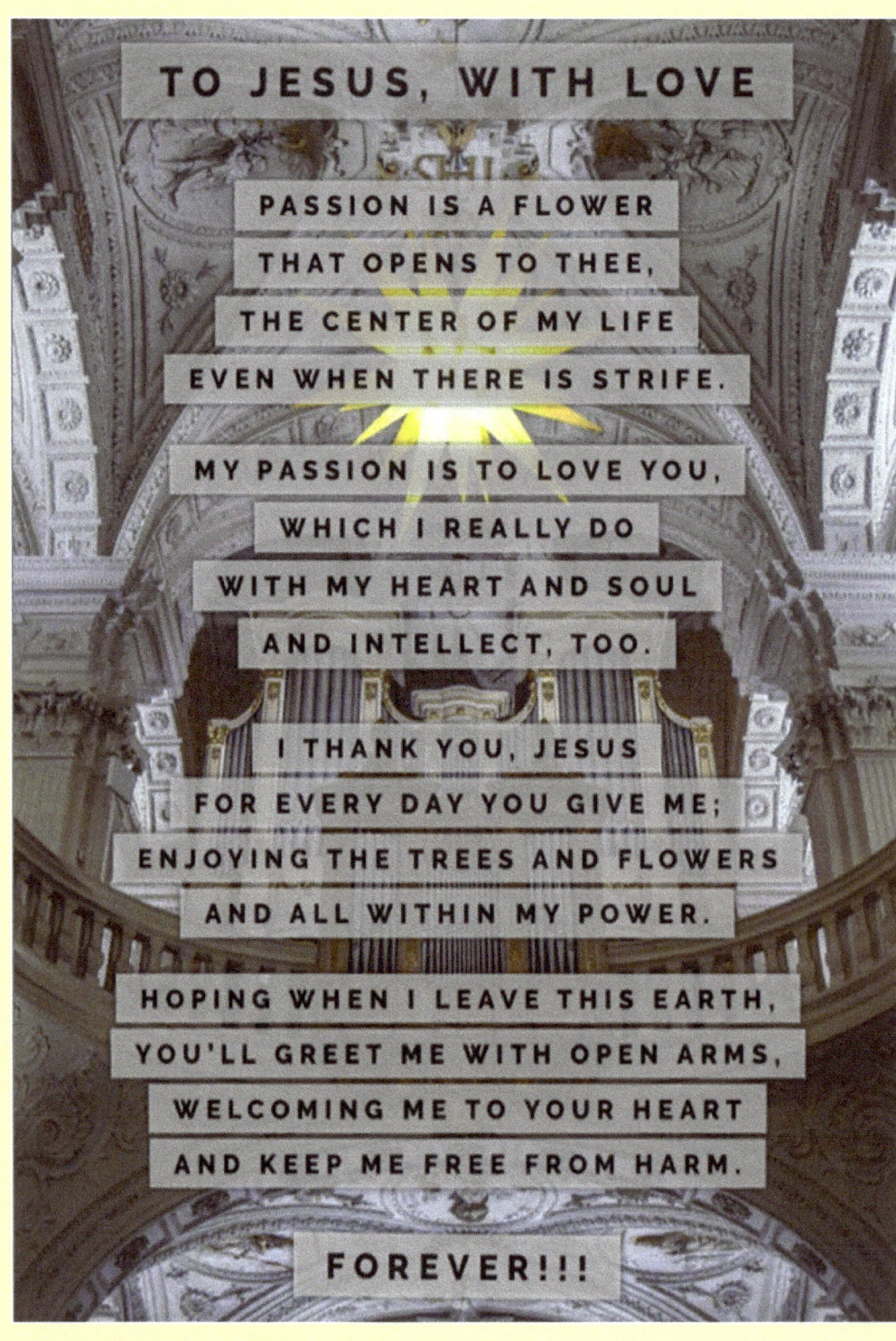

TO JESUS, WITH LOVE

PASSION IS A FLOWER
THAT OPENS TO THEE,
THE CENTER OF MY LIFE
EVEN WHEN THERE IS STRIFE.

MY PASSION IS TO LOVE YOU,
WHICH I REALLY DO
WITH MY HEART AND SOUL
AND INTELLECT, TOO.

I THANK YOU, JESUS
FOR EVERY DAY YOU GIVE ME;
ENJOYING THE TREES AND FLOWERS
AND ALL WITHIN MY POWER.

HOPING WHEN I LEAVE THIS EARTH,
YOU'LL GREET ME WITH OPEN ARMS,
WELCOMING ME TO YOUR HEART
AND KEEP ME FREE FROM HARM.

FOREVER!!!

Forgiveness

SOMETIMES WE SPEAK
NOT KNOWING THE CONSEQUENCES IT BRINGS.
HURTING SOMEONE'S FEELINGS
SHOULD NOT BE OUR THING.

GOD FROWNS ON OUR WORDS,
WHICH SHOULD BE GIVING US GRIEF,
AND THROUGH OUR BELIEF
OUR CONSCIENCE IS HEARD.

GUILTY FEELINGS ARISE
FOR WHAT WE HAVE SAID.
THEN WE ASK FOR FORGIVENESS
FROM GOD AND OUR FRIEND.

FACES

HEAVENLY FATHER,

I SEE SO MANY FACES
IN SO MANY PLACES.
WHY ARE THEY STARING AT ME?

I TRY TO BE GOOD,
BUT SOMETIMES, I'M BAD.
IS THIS WHY THE FACES LOOK SO SAD?

HELP ME

OH, LORD! WILL YOU HELP ME
WITH A PROBLEM I HAVE?
MY PATIENCE GETS THIN
WHEN A PREDICAMENT, I'M IN.

I KNOW PATIENCE IS A VIRTUE
WITH WHICH I'M NOT BLESSED.
SO, I APPEAL FROM THE HEART,
GIVE MY LIFE A NEW START.

AT TIMES, I CAN'T COPE,
BUT I'LL ALWAYS HAVE HOPE
THAT WHEN EACH DAY, I PRAY,
YOU'LL SEND PATIENCE MY WAY.

THOUGHTS ON THE LORD'S PRAYER

OUR FATHER WHO ART IN HEAVEN,
In my human mind, what do I see?
The Lord, looking down on you & me.

HALLOWED BE THY NAME.
God, the father of us all.

THY KINGDOM COME,
Sitting on a bench in a great hall.

THY WILL BE DONE
We should, but don't always,
do as You say.

ON EARTH, AS IT IS IN HEAVEN.
Every single day.

GIVE US THIS DAY OUR DAILY BREAD.
Some have, but others don't.

AND FORGIVE US OUR TRESPASSES,
  Bad things we think, do, or say
  should not be our way.

**AS WE FORGIVE THOSE WHO
TRESPASS AGAINST US.**
  With words or deeds.
  Leave us alone, they won't.

LEAD US NOT INTO TEMPTATION,
  Keep us from acting on
  some of our choices.

BUT DELIVER US FROM EVIL.
  Let me be safe from
  all the sources.

AMEN
  I love You, God, the Father,
  and Jesus, your Son.

Giggles

The Fly in the Sky

The fly in the sky was so tiny,
you couldn't even see his hiney.

He flew all around—
where a car ran him over
and he ended up in clover.

No one saw him there
with his feet in the air,
pointing to the sky—
where the fly used to be.

A FACE IN THE TREE

A FACE IN THE TREE
NOW, WHO COULD IT BE?
LOOK REALLY HARD,
AND YOU WILL SEE,
A FACE IN THE TREE.

IT'S NOT VERY BIG
AND IT'S NOT VERY SMALL.
MEDIUM SIZE—
IS THAT FACE IN THE TREE.

I SEE A MOUTH
AND I SEE A NOSE.
I SEE EYES THAT GROW AND GROW.

I THINK IT'S AN OWL,
DO YOU AGREE?
OF THAT FACE CARVED IN THE TREE.

THE BRIGHT LIGHT

Pat, with her forehead so shiny and red,
May have to help guide Santa's sled.
In front of all the reindeer, it will be so dark,
But with all the light it will be a bright lark.

Santa asked, "Pat, how will this work?"
We thought and thought, and then with a smirk,
Rudolph said, "Come ride on my back,
As it will be soft with hay in a sack."

The thrill was there, riding high in the sky,
Pat never imagined she'd be able to fly.
The double light was so bright
That Santa had no trouble with his sight.

Coming in for a landing,
In the sled, he was standing.
But suddenly, dogs started barking
Because of the light when Santa was parking.
Santa called out, "Quick, cover your forehead,
And cover your nose,
Or the people will come out with a hose!"

Suddenly, Pat said, "This has been so much fun,
But now I must run.
Good-bye my friends, Rudolph and Santa,
Maybe it's best if you use some lanterns."

& More

LONELINESS

I MOVED TO A NEW HOME,
WHERE I'M QUITE CONTENT
BUT SOMETIMES THE LONELINESS HAS ME SPENT.

I TRY TO KEEP BUSY,
BUT HOUSEWORK MAKES ME DIZZY.

THE YARD IS A MESS
AS THE GRASS KEEPS ON GROWING.
SO, WEEKLY, I HAVE TO DO THE MOWING.

I HAVE MET SOME PEOPLE
WHO ARE QUITE FRIENDLY,
BUT AT TIMES, LONELINESS IS A MEDLEY.

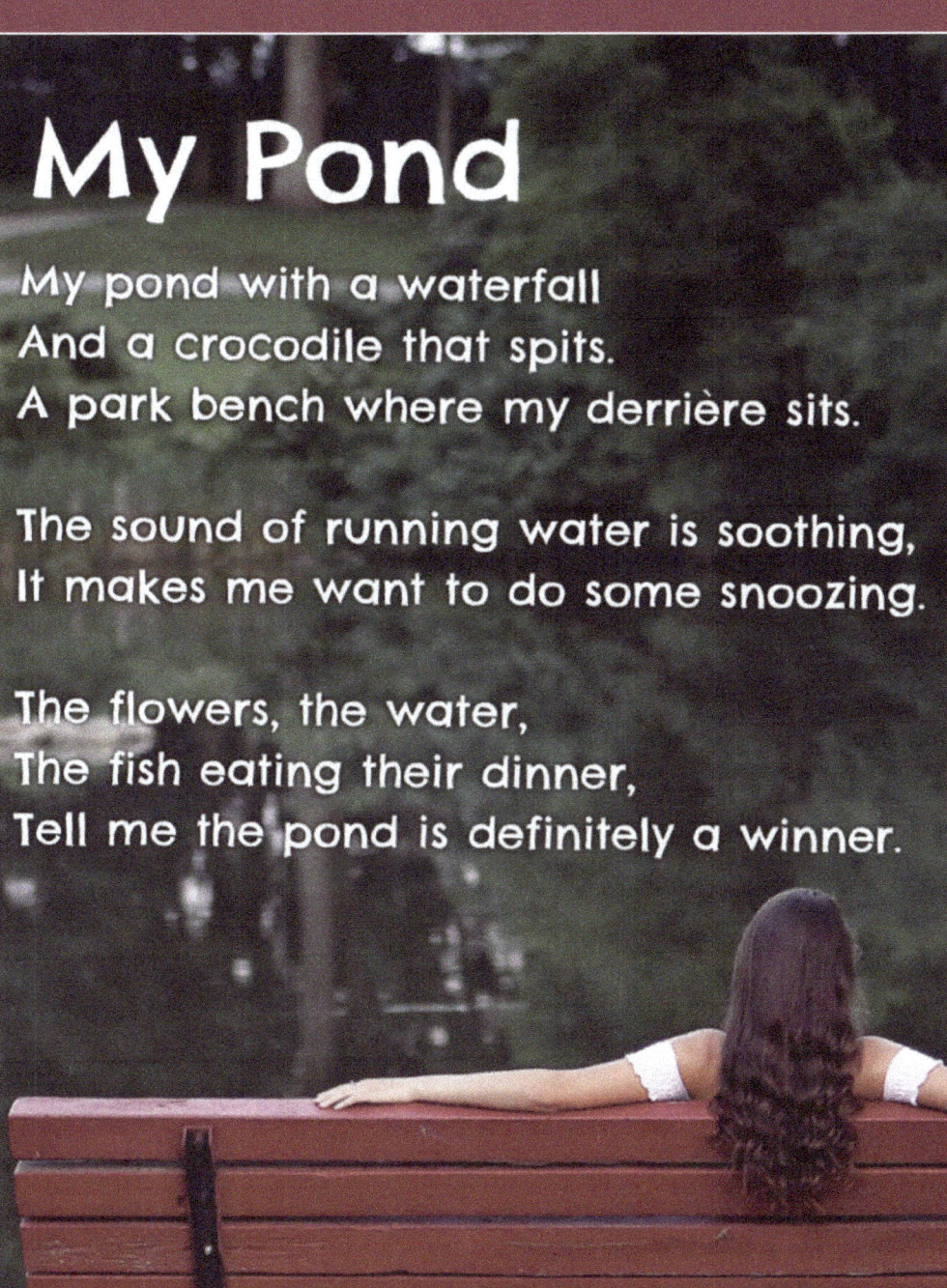

My Pond

My pond with a waterfall
And a crocodile that spits.
A park bench where my derrière sits.

The sound of running water is soothing,
It makes me want to do some snoozing.

The flowers, the water,
The fish eating their dinner,
Tell me the pond is definitely a winner.

I WANT TO BE FREE

I WANT TO BE A BIRD IN A TREE,
A BUTTERFLY LANDING ON A KNEE.

A BEE SIPPING NECTAR FROM A FLOWER,
AN EAGLE SOARING WITH GREAT POWER.

I WANT TO BE A DOLPHIN IN THE SEA,
CAVORTING WHERE PEOPLE, ON LAND, CAN SEE.

A SEAGULL ON THE BEACH,
WITH FOOD THROWN WITHIN MY REACH.

SO, AS YOU CAN SEE,

I WANT TO BE FREE!

THE GOLDEN YEARS

MY KNEES ARE SO WEAK,
MY HEARING IS BAD.
MY MIND GETS ADDLED,
WHICH MAKES ME SAD.

I LOOK IN THE MIRROR,
WHO CAN THAT BE?
ALL THOSE WRINKLES,
IT'S CERTAINLY NOT ME.

MY HAIR IS SNOW WHITE.
MY TEETH ARE A LIGHT YELLOW.
I STARE AT SOME MAN,
WHO IS THAT FELLOW?

WHEN MY MIND GETS CLEAR,
I KNOW IT'S MY SPOUSE
A LONG, LONG TIME
LIVING IN THIS HOUSE.

WITH ALL OF OUR DREAMS
WE'RE TOGETHER AS ONE.
WHERE HAVE THE YEARS GONE,
SINCE WE WERE YOUNG?

THE GOLDEN YEARS,
I REALLY THINK NOT.
WITH MANY ACHES AND PAINS,
THEY'RE NOT SO HOT.

GOOD TIMES, THERE ARE,
I SURELY AGREE.
BUT YOU WILL SEE
WHEN YOU'RE AS OLD AS ME.

Acknowledgments

I would like to extend a special thank you to my friend, Ingrid Cathell, at Pathway Writings, for her professional guidance and creativity.

A big thank you to my pastor and friend, Mark Erskine, who has critiqued many of my writings. His input has been invaluable, which has helped me grow as a writer.

www.ingramcontent.com/pod-product-compliance
Lightning Source LLC
Chambersburg PA
CBHW042337040426
42446CB00021B/3481